THE SILENCE OF DOORWAYS

THE SILENCE OF DOORWAYS

poems by
Sharon Venezio

Foreword by Dorothy Barresi

Moon Tide Press

March 2013

The Silence of Doorways

Editors
Ricki Mandeville
Michael Miller

Graphic design
Michael Wada

Front cover art
Marsel Van Oosten

Back cover photo
Carmel France

Moon Tide logo design
Ricki Mandeville

The Silence of Doorways
is published by
Moon Tide Press
Irvine, California
www.moontidepress.com

Website designed by Mindy Nettifee and John Turi

FIRST EDITION

Printed in the United States of America

ISBN # 978-0-9839651-5-2

CONTENTS

FOREWORD

Sharon Venezio's terrific first collection of poems, *The Silence of Doorways*, reminds us that the best new poetry—the kind we delight in reading—is nimble in its negotiations between assurance and surprise, wit and discovery, sense and transcendence. It entices but will not lead. It does not vamp or mug or advertise or campaign. Its meanings are at once multiple and protean, and our likely satisfaction in those meanings has no money-back guarantee, because the best new poetry must taunt and defy and reveal and intensify. It unseats; it stubbornly refuses to yield, then unexpectedly, it demurs, becomes gold. It changes as we change. It feels as though it were always necessary. "Speech is the distinguishing feature of civilization if you want to avoid annihilation open your mouth and sing," Venezio writes. The best new poetry, like so many of the astonishingly assured pieces herein, pries open language's possibility without using the crowbar of blunt metaphor. They never clang shut on interpretation or show off their own—ta da!—brilliance, either, but instead are deft, even delicate, in their refusal of easy answers. Venezio knows how to let language find its own strange freshness, and her poems ache with a yearning for human connection that refuses sentimentality, as in "Studying for the MCAT":

> *Lungs, you say, are the unimagined house*
> *inside the body, the breathing universe*
> *with the breadth of snow and silence*
>
> *and the trachea is a lonely brown thrasher*
> *singing the longest love song in history.*
> *We lie in bed, gaze at the phosphorescent*
>
> *stars stuck to the ceiling and wall,*
> *constellations collide with the dresser,*
> *the cat appears to wear the rings of Saturn.*
>
> *This duplicate sky is alive and burning*
> *more bright than nature,*
> *more true to imagination.*

The best new poetry is alive to momentary joy and nearly overwhelming doubt and loneliness—the building blocks of life now or anytime! It reminds us that nothing in human experience (not even the "fixed" image of a photograph—one of Venezio's central tropes for the past as associated with the speaker's disappointed and emotionally withdrawn father as well as a brother who is both deeply loved and lost, perhaps to drugs) can be read in singular array, but is, like memory, a shifting, shaded, highly volatile composition. "My eyelid is a shutter / that opens to receive the day so beautiful / it must be a lie," she writes in "Now We Become Ghosts." One after another, Venezio's poems in their postmodern wariness of unmediated experience ask not whether we can know anything for sure (we can't), but how we might make ourselves more fully and deeply human even now, in the jaws of this new virtual century. That is, how we might love without the distancing defenses and ironies of the terminally hip.

After the rain stops,
birds flood the courtyard,
swooping the air
with what seems like joy.

We watch through
the kitchen window,
a bowl of curried vegetables
on the table.

The air outside
pulses with pleasure.
It's hard to say
what makes us happiest.

The food? The wings
that open without fear?
Or the rest of our life
that flies in and in and in.

Loss is at the heart of *The Silence of Doorways*, as is its twin, desire: for reassurance, for succor, for love, for liberation. For self knowledge ("I am not bird song, not feeder, not seed / not sun rising on unripe blueberries. I am / not a deer head mounted on the hunter's wall, / not the tiny body lifted onto her uncle's / shoulders to caress the carcass, /

finger the wildly dead black eyes"). For a way to close and protect the broken family, and when it is understood that that cannot be done ("The underbelly of family / is the color of ash, / a face afraid of mirrors") for a way to reach beyond the closed-off, wounded self. The best new poetry still gives, yes, a sense of sudden liberation, but it also places one more polished stone of desire onto the endless pile of stones we erect each day inside ourselves. It is, dare I say it, always existential: self-centered, concerned with survival in its most intimate sense *as* meaning, and that meaning in turn is panoramic, generous, instructive, exploratory, a bridge. If we are lucky, new poetry tells us something we need to know about our own lives, in our own voice. In *The Silence of Doorways*, we recognize the territory but the map is made beautifully new.

—Dorothy Barresi

"The camera relieves us of the burden of memory."
—John Berger

I

Landscapes

OBSESSION \äb-'sesh-ən, əb-\
n.

1. If he touches the table once, she will leave him. If he touches the table twice, she will stay. Even numbers have the power to stop death; odd numbers rot the brain.

2. If he speaks for her, she learns to keep her lips still, the shutters slid shut. If not talking is a kind of death, he has killed her. A cluster of numbers rotting in the throat.

3. Spring does not replenish their lives, though the yard is alive with Hyacinth, birds swollen with song. A digital hunter, he comes and goes with his camera, returning with a piece of nature, captured.

4. Everything under the arc of routine, even spring with flowers planted four inches apart. If he plants an odd number, he won't survive winter.

5. When he dies, will birds fold their wings in grief?

6. If only the world were innumerable.

COLLEGE ESSAY

for Deshika

Is it just that I'm leaving home or has my bedroom always been this beautiful? My walls are earthy green. A black and white print of Audrey Hepburn hangs above the piano, magazine faces stare out from the closet wall, and there are words sketched in Sharpie on my desk; each space a contradiction. I can't draw, but if I could for my mother a sketch of Van Gogh's Almond Blossoms with their soft hesitant life for all her looking inward, and for my father a picture of a red fronted macaw perched on the cliffs of Bolivia for all his looking outward.

My brother is a Buddhist. He's 23, says he will soon live in the forest in Sri Lanka, like a monk. He will name flowers, then unname them. He will not contact our mother. The bird in his heart does not feel hunger; it closes its soundless wings and dreams. He doesn't like his ego, tries to kill it nightly in his room. My ego would like to go to your college. I will call my mother every day. One day I will visit Sri Lanka, find my brother sitting somewhere in the Sri Pada wilderness, bring him food, tell him all I have learned at your college. He will tell me to forget it all, and I will.

PSYCHOLOGY 402: BRAIN AND BEHAVIOR

When I discover I have to dissect a sheep's brain,
I go down the hall to Animal Behavior and plead my case,
but it's too late. I'll have to pry my way through
the four ventricles, push pins into gray matter and breathe
formaldehyde through a useless white mask.

I hold the brain in my awful hands, make an incision
at the base of the cerebellum, place a red pin
into the pineal gland, a green pin into the amygdala:
here's where it feels joy, here's where it feels fear,
here's where it remembers the beautiful dying stars.

NOW WE BECOME GHOSTS

When I moved to the west coast,
my father, a street smart storyteller
who read only one book
(the biography of JFK)
said "don't trust anyone."

He trusted the birds
perched on the backyard feeder,
red throated above the grass
that gleamed with our weeping.

He trusted his camera to capture
nightjar, thrush, swallow,
refrigerated grasshopper
a perfect still life until it warmed.

His mother came from Ireland on a boat,
twelve, motherless, not even a bird to trust,
erasing her name in the frozen cave
of her heart.

Now, as the aperture of morning
expands over California,
my father is a ghost in my camera lens
collecting variations of light.

My eyelid is a shutter
that opens to receive the day
so beautiful
it must be a lie.

PHOTOGRAPHER

He sits behind lens for hours in darkness,
waiting for the first fleck of sun, first wing to span.
He is not cold in the cold. He is shuttered, apertured.

When he was a boy he watched
enormous morning light stretch across the sky,
and its beauty was enough.

Now, an osprey's hungry mouth
swooping the dark surface says *sadness.*
A hatchling sea turtle, hurrying across the tideline
into its 1 in 1000 chance of survival, *grief.*

IMPRINT

I notice an imprint of a bird on the office window,
a perfect outline of the face. My finger traces
the still pool of the eyes, the creased, anonymous forehead.

From the edge of my wingless day, I imagine
her nesting, delivering mouthfuls of food
to craving young, swooping down,

coming back again. I close my eyes,
wish for rain to erode the uncommissioned canvas
of the winged and windowed, the sparrowed and swallowed,

and to wash me, too, out of this workday into the vast skyline,
away from the men who hover five stories high
who squeegee her imploded beak, blindly erase her eyes.

STUDYING FOR THE MCAT

Lungs, you say, are the unimagined house
inside the body, the breathing universe
with the breadth of snow and silence

and the trachea is a lonely brown thrasher
singing the longest love song in history.
We lie in bed, gaze at the phosphorescent

stars stuck to the ceiling and wall,
constellations collide with the dresser,
the cat appears to wear the rings of Saturn.

This duplicate sky is alive and burning
more bright than nature,
more true to imagination.

The heart, I say, is a false sunflower
sprouting from your cupped human hand.

II

Single Exposure

MEANWHILE, AN OBSESSION

i

meanwhile your belly insistent the curve itself insinuates all directions your breasts flush in my mouth lungs expelling your voice like a tendril ascending throat contracts turns upward in beautiful movement the cruelest of monsters I gather you up in pieces

ii

a female voice corresponds to three halftones below middle C a male voice registers one octave and a halftone below middle C speech is the distinguishing feature of civilization if you want to avoid annihilation open your mouth and sing

iii

fortune-tellers midwives healers the seventeenth century brought no relief legal torture permits sadistic experimentation and gratuitous sexual acts when Catherine was raped and murdered in her cell blame was placed on the devil science as yet can make no determination

iv

love is an infection she said the two women I love are dead taken flight taken wing her own hand betraying the body tearing what time is left what time is flesh a day's work is death the only form of respect she knows and does not know bird on the side of the road smashed up stream of cars fluttering by

v

the ovum is immobile and waits passively always in bed the sky opening above me an obsession this counting the stars burning holes in the sky I spin my nest gripped by the unentering simply to accept the page I'm reading the words before me the dying

vi

I have lived with refusal emotional distance across bodies a brilliant subjugation loyalty to the body marveled and admired by all a spectacle of evolution an institutional subject-position holds no vacancy the currency of discourse tufts of hair warm spine a circle will lead nowhere please talk in a straight line

vii

an ongoing process by which subjectivity is constructed semiotically bodily experience though seemingly immediate is socially mediated never discrete nominal essences are often treated as if they were real this is the main point of vulnerability his hands on my face while inscribing a brand new class to locate and contain the subject

viii

sick of pulling at the sky of myself and this restless mirror like a raven beating on this cold smooth pane a vague impression he thinks he might remember my name he tells me I look unhappy his face a primordial fossil a roar from deep within I open my mouth and howl

ix

the text plunges into abstraction is annihilated by contradiction a room of used furniture he laughs at her but one expects that in marriage only 417 whooping cranes left on earth Charlie is part of a new experiment whooper chicks raised by humans it is imperative he believes he is wild if you recall the flutter the beating the wing

x

hunters wait until dawn or dusk and they lure their prey with decoys most birds don't make their first migration the woman opens a window her baby wailing and wild there are many shadows in the room woman is a migrating shadow stimming bird mouth whooping at the sky

III

Portraits

A GEOGRAPHY IN FRAGMENTS

i
arrival

the berry tree is buried in snow
hovering over a coldness

the yard is a mirror

my bird heart flapping in its cage
hands filled with winter

it's all I've managed so far
snow and wind and fingers

a clear blue ice
spreads over the yard

nothing is young anymore

ii
we have a slide show in the basement
my mother makes popcorn for the kids
they call it a *movie*

projected stills
of all that is left of wild america

elk
bison
moose

the grand tetons
the zion narrows

balancing on algae-coated rocks
in the middle of a swiftly flowing river

my father with his camera
a good hunter

GHOST BROTHER

Six
The human figures confuse me.
Father's fist drums down
on the ghost, though he doesn't
fight back.

His bruised body limp
in our father's hands.
My mouth burning.

Eight
The underbelly of family
is the color of ash,
a face afraid of mirrors.

The ghost calls me to him
at the age of eight

watches me watch him
as he jumps off the roof
into the pool.

Twelve
The ghost invites me
into his room, swaying,
playing a song on the guitar.
Swaying like the ragged
willow that floats
in the dark window.

Out of touch with the rhythm
of the music, heroin eyes
spinning like the turntable,
wrong lyrics, wrong note,
and he wants me to watch.

Fourteen
The ghost stole mother's
jewelry. Half-moon diamond
and bloodstone.

The ring our father saved
for months to buy.
Money earned sweating
over a machine, doing things
he never intended
his hands to do.

Fifteen
The ghost is an empty mouth,
opening and closing, empty
chair at the dinner table,
empty eyes floating in his face,
ghost chanting:
Look at me, I'm nothing.
Do you want to be like me?

POLAROID

That morning it was the Marlboro cigarette
I stole from my brother's ashtray,
a lock on the upstairs bathroom door
where I exhaled the letter o
out the little window.

That afternoon it was the dumb stillness,
a handful of pills I thieved
from his pale green jar.

The night would be arsenic in the o
of my mouth.

FROM A BAR IN ELIZABETH, NEW JERSEY

have to pretend
i am someone else
someone who smiles
while she pours drinks
tilts the bottle just right
so the liquor flirts
with the air
on the way into the glass
a foot and a half of formica
defines our role
all night they mine
my face for a clue
think i am someone
they can love
slur their dedications
in half-light
by midnight
cocaine's stimming
bird mouth
whoops at winter sky
through open door
this helps them
pretend they are
someone else
forget the snow
piling up on hoods
of cars forget the children
sheeted in beds
sleep wrapped around
their bright bodies

NOVA

My first car
cost 500 dollars.
'76 Chevy Nova,
dirt brown.

Jiggle handle to open,
turn engine three times
to start.

It was more beautiful
than salt air,
ocean, wing.

It was passage,
shift, spark.

The bone-dry
squeaky waste land,
where life began.

Brown Nova had no past,
only the moon's
emerging promise.

STORM

1.
In the slack of home, the TV was always on.

Children safe in their pajamas, housed
in a cul-de-sac of blue-lit windows.

Drying the last dish, her work was done.
She will go on like this for decades.

2.
A round wood table
where food turns

the people into a family

look how beautiful
their grievance.

3.
Her husband stands
in a field with his camera

shutter open to the flood
of light.

He photographs birds,
knows their names
and habits.

She measures the distance
between wife and lens,

migrates inward.

4.
The storm was like the sky
overflowing, spilling into windows

but more like a storm.

Like a storm
overflowing into windows

the windows
                              open out
onto the unstoppable world

5.
There is an ancient sorrow
tattooed on her chest
buoyant as a lifejacket.

She can no longer feel
the boundary
between her body
and the water.

RETURNING

1. My Mother is a House

Inside my mother
there's an unspooling
of afghans, a sewing machine

(she sews the day shut;
her needle works the silence),

a Dewey Decimal System
of socks and pajamas.

For years I stared
out her window,
said fuck you to the flowers.

2. My Father is a Bird

In the morning
the birds are so loud
they wake me.

He tells stories all day,
cuts bread into tiny squares,
scatters it over the backyard grass.

I watch for a flame of wings.
I will be a murmuration,
that flap flap flap of sky.

UPON FURTHER REFLECTION

there is a kitchen inside her

where she cooks meal
after meal   but never eats

she is a green bowl
stacked high with nothing

a tea cup
hanged & hooked

her face   not wet with sun

SNAPSHOT IN SEPIA

I
Years ago, my mother closed her bedroom window
and never looked out again. She collapsed like a wave
folding inward. She said *hope can be an anchor;*
it's easier to just let go.

I was fourteen and just barely paying attention,
straddling Billy's bike seat
while he pedaled standing up.

As the world turned on the grainy screen
of my mother's TV, Billy and I watched leaves
circle down from the maple outside my bedroom window.
They'd land on the hood of the orange Cutlass,
gather like unopened letters.

II
Our house had a crawl space
we entered through a removable bookcase in the wall.
I'd scale suitcases and boxes of family photos
until I reached the end. I'd draw a window on the wall,

open it up, let the pretend breeze pour
over my face and body
like my mother in her secret life
breathing the salt air of the sea.

Now I stand at the edge of the ocean
scatter her memory like a constellation
splayed across the night sky,
like moonlight unstitching the stars.

FAMILY ALBUM

Here a cigarette dangles between her thin fingers;
she sleeps through conversation and ash.
Here she closes her eyes and the sea stops moving.

And here she is a boneyard of unspoken words,
salt in the quiet throat of her marriage.
Here she is the green whiff of childhood.

Here she is sparrowed at the edge of the earth,
exiled in her dying skin. Here, like sorrow,
she is liquid in the bones.

And here is the day she will be gone, her eyes resting
no longer upon the tulips, their white
petals, like teeth, fall to the ground.

Here she is hair, and nail, and noise in the brain.
And here, dear body, be still. Time is the only lover
that will touch her now.

MOTHER

Every poem about a mother
is its own sorrow, its own white iris
looking out at the world.
Ted's geese resting in the pond,
peonies burning circles in the sky.

Mary's mother is blue wisteria,
a mossy stream behind her house
brings order to the world.
She tells us to live with the beetle
and the wind, to let life untidy us.

My mother didn't like to be in nature,
but she took great care of her plants,
knew their language, smoothed
the dark veins of their leaves.
Her poem will not contain flowers,

no wisteria, no iris delivered
from the house of the dead.
I'll call it Poem with Its Head in Its Hands
and there will be an artichoke,
its thirsty shape urging us

to unbrace its layered heart.
Her husband will call it
Be the Flame, Renew My Thirst.
Her son will call it
The Darkness Is Not Here to Stay.

IV

Multiple Exposures

WATER ASKS A QUESTION

after Nick Flynn

in the streets they're dancing
for the dead, I mean the killing

they're killing for the dead
but there will still be water
& throat & hose

dead eyes and photographs
to shame the living.

we arrive, sandbags
over our heads, beat naked
kneel & squat & click & click

o sky o chain
o clothes beat broken

hang me to the door
open my mouth
to not speak

ABU GHRAIB

3 a.m. soldier, my bedroom, my children, my head,
my hands heard screaming, next a cage, a tent.

one month and just before sunset
flooded with water and waste

cut our hearts under his tongue, body away.
lost hearing lost consciousness lost mind.

sometimes spark sometimes spread sometimes click
sometimes water sometimes drown

they said pose they said smile they said sing
rope wrist rope pipe rope hours

do you? did you? do you recognize this fist?

POEMS OF SUBMISSION

after James L White

1. Submission to the Present

The trouble with the past
is that it creeps up on you.

I've been dying to crawl inside
the photos, to breathe the smell
of when things were new,

to sit across from your warbling mind,
your whooping crane mouth,
to watch you rise like a flame of swallows.

Dear Future: there's no way back.

2. Submission to Your Touch

I'd rather watch someone do it on TV
or read a monologue about it.

I want to sit in the shrinking light
of my own body, which is separate
from your body.

Here is a photograph to tape to my face.
Here is one for my belly.
And one with a hole in the middle.

Can you find me?

THREE EXITS

after Nathalie Handal

Version One

Place a story in her ear,
be the salt on the back of her tongue.
Make too much noise.
Say goodbye, forget her name,
don't take a picture.

Version Two

Take a picture, write her name
on the back with a green gel pen,
slip it into your bag,
glance back
as you close the door.

Version Three

Say goodbye, but never leave.
Let night tell you who you are.
Unbutton her face, be the green thorn
piercing the small furious flap of her heart.

STILL LIFE

after David Biespiel

After the rain stops,
birds flood the courtyard,
swooping the air
with what seems like joy.

We watch through
the kitchen window,
a bowl of curried vegetables
on the table.

The air outside
pulses with pleasure.
It's hard to say
what makes us happiest.

The food? The wings
that open without fear?
Or the rest of our life
that flies in and in and in.

SO FAR

after Olena Kalytiak Davis

So far, have come this far.
a cat, some books.
So far, an ocean.

So far, cicadas still slip
into dreams.
So far, love, have managed.

So far, a love like panic,
eluded and elapsed.
So far, in love with lack.

So far, a box of letters,
blank as paper.
So far, still burns.

POEMS FOR FREUD

1. POEM OF EGO

after Evie Shockley

Self-portrait with cat, with books
organized by genre and size,
with Rothko, with earth tones,
with coffee and no cigarettes.

Self-portrait with light and shadow,
with paroxetine, with butternut squash
and Napa red, with half-read,
with hipster friends too young to know.

Self-portrait with defense mechanisms,
with wild delphinium, with flophouse
hybrid bleeding heart, with howling mouth
and listening moon. Self-portrait as you.

2. POEM OF EROS & THANATOS

after Kevin Prufer

Photographing the world
from the driver's seat
of an air conditioned car
is not the best way to fall in love.

A good way to fall in love
is to drive ten miles over the limit
with no seatbelt,

or ride in a hot air balloon
over Temecula shouting poems
to the vineyards below,

or plant words like seeds,
watch them rise.

A good way to fall in love
is to have nothing left to say,
to let fog envelop the day
like diazepam,

or swallow a bottle of quiet
white pills and wait
for the bright hush of night.

3. POEM OF DENIAL

I am not my young mother in her apron,
blazed with anticipation. I am not half shadow,
not waiting unanchored in the shifting.

I am not bird song, not feeder, not seed,
not sun rising on unripe blueberries.
I am not a deer head

mounted on the hunter's wall, not the tiny body
lifted onto her uncle's shoulders to caress
the carcass, finger the wildly dead black eyes.

4. POEM OF UNDOING

How many kinds of undoing are there?
The word love in the back of the throat,
mouth ajar, as I don't say your name?

My heart is a thirsty artichoke,
each petal a different version of undoing.

V

Over Exposures

[UNTITLED]
To Francesca Woodman

where do you end and the world begin?

you want to be wind   vapor
half flower   half vase

wallpaper   tree bark   door
you become line   shape

you invisible the self

we raise our eyelids to your frame

in this one your nakedness crawls
toward a white calla   you bend

into our looking   watch us shift
in our seat   as the lens eats you

you are a brief installation of curved
bone and wall

jumping from a window
you are both sidewalk   and falling

did you think the camera would catch you?

BECOMING THE IMAGE

look how she introduces herself
wearing only black shoes

her body merges with the wall
the story is not the body, not
the wall, but the merging

the mirrors and windows can't
believe their own surfaces

the untellable outline of what is

a woman is
a reflection eaten by light
flattened by paper

the gesture of a camera in her hand
constructor and constructed

every glance speaking
the unspoken body
a sliver of mirror   on and on

SELF-PORTRAIT AS CAMERA

When I was young
I was just a pinhole projection
of an upside-down world.

I struggled to get a fixed image,
to not disappear.

My shuttered lens opening
like a tiny mirror,
like the hungry aperture of light.

TURNING 41

It's like turning 31, only worse.
It's like looking for ghosts over my shoulder
while the conversation swerves into its third drink.
It's like you're watching me from your grave
asking me how I survived.

I remember the year you ran away,
hitchhiked to Florida, became a Deadhead,
the year I learned emptiness can settle inside
a teenage body.

Each night I watched the moon.
Each night I closed my eyes
to make it disappear.

A BRIEF MOMENT OF FLIGHT

talking to Sartre in the shower,
I forget to wash my hair. this is the first of my mistakes.

if hell is other people, then heaven must be solitude,
and nothing is an atheist's paradise.

perhaps Descartes was right:
even bodies are not properly known by the senses

I thought of myself first as having a face   hands   arms
which I designated by the name of body.

a body occupies space
in such a way
that every other body
is excluded from it.

remember: *I am. I exist.*
thought is an attribute that belongs to me.
I am not a wind, a flame, a breath, a vapor,
or anything at all.

sometimes Picasso's Bird Woman is all I can see,
wings flapping in my eyes

a chorus of voices
                    suspended in the spine

and another day spent inside,
infinitely removed from every kind of perfection,

each thought demanding its own location,
a streetsign, an interstate.

anguish is evident even when it conceals itself.
all the untying and untying for a brief moment of flight.

ADDERALL

It was an experiment for my nephew's sake,
an act of empathy. I wanted to know
what it was like for him, only twelve.

I'd witnessed the results, compared the pre
and post. He was a thought rising with poise,
then slouching off the page,

a series of feral letters. Then he was legible,
contained, assembled into meaning.
He needed a zoom lens, and there it was,

a round blue pill, a clean line of focus.
The letters finally making sense.

Perhaps it wasn't empathy that brought
the pill to my mouth. That day
was statistics class, a mush of numbers,

equations. The professor's determined
hands dusted with chalk. The numbers
finally making sense.

Stillness is a landscape, a soft blue drift.
Attention is a sharp red circle,
mind ablaze with watching.

It grips your chin in the palm of its hand,
like a parent, turns your head, says: *look at this.*

NUMEROSITIES

I don't know if I slid the patio door shut,
pushed the lever down to lock it, so I'll drive
3 miles back home, check 2 more times.

So many monkeys swinging from my neurobranches,
counting the nerves bundled above the left ear,
the blazing apple that compels enumeration.

It takes 500 calories a day to grow neurotransmitters,
0 calories to recognize the greenness of a leaf,
the twoness of two, the threeness of three.

Numbers kept my father's hands moving,
always digging 4 inches deep, 12 inches apart,
arriving 8 minutes early, his mind monkey

juggling evens and odds. My mother counts
the teaspoons of sugar for her tea, the minutes
while the water boils.

Meanwhile, I count the number
of steps out of a movie theatre
so I can count my way back through the dark.

DISQUIETUDE

for Dushan

For two months I've been living with monks.
No longer dizzy from the circle of worry,
I see truth in the order of things,
eat for the body, not the senses. Still

I crave the sky in my mouth, feel
Kerouac's fabulous roman candles explode
like spiders beneath my skin, wake

yawning for coffee, daydream
of curry and spice, make poems in my head
about the wild dishevelment of being,
that fierce blue drowning.

Of the ten defilements, passion is the one
I can't shake. In a month, I'll step out
of the forest, carry my longing home again.

WINTER

I

O how you follow me around campus,
leave couplets on my windshield:

Love, if you love me, lie next to me. Be for me like rain,
be wet with a decent happiness.

We fall in love in the coffee shop
over books and Italian dark roast.

The days are large. You speak with your hands
in the air. You say my name out loud.

II
For years we're happy, even after I leave
for San Francisco. We watch the meteor shower,

you in Los Angeles, your voice in my ear
directs me toward the light.

Gazing into our shared darkness,
we're tethered by sky, by cosmic debris.

Time accumulates into a hundred moons,
whiteness begins to drift down from the sky.

III
Every morning the same view,
open your eyes, nothing to see

but white everywhere. Your mind becomes
an unfamiliar constellation and I cannot

compel clarity, cannot force reason upon you.
Too soon frost will kill the paper white narcissus,

leaving a continent of nothing, only the winged
and shadowed yowling at the sky.

IV
Like a burned out house, there is nothing to return to.
You are both dead and not dead, not the future,

only the past suspended in time. Your illness
buries the days under a cage of snow.

But winter is a time of waiting, so I wait,
revise myself again and again, follow the moon's

nightly migration, the way it loses itself
only to begin again, a constant return.

A MAY ELEGY
for R.B.

Turn the knob and walk in.
The house is empty

except for the animals,
who have been waiting

and are still. Light stretches
across your unmade bed

projecting patterns
of universe on the wall.

The planets call your name,
my heart turns on its axis.

Perhaps you never existed
and those years were stolen from me.

But your desk holds evidence of you,
littered with guidebooks:

How to Maintain
a Salt Water Tank

An Introduction
to North American Snakes

The pages are silent.
It is April,

your ghost face
postered on every telephone pole,

bones sniffed out by a dog
on the corner of Oldham Lane.

Your death is a hole in the earth
where your heart fell through.

From your memory, I make seeds,
sun. I fill my lungs with light,

even when the white sheet sky of winter
will not fold back.

THE FLAME

Night's wingspan, wide as moon,
stretches toward the horizon.
Your ghost is an unkindness

of ravens contained like a photograph
moody with shadow. Your ghost
is an ancient tree

with nests of hair that flame
white hibiscus, the flowers still bloom
the garden with light.

Each fall I eat the flowered flame
to forget you, petal by petal,
eat it down to its grief

o doomed lover
hold your face up to the sky
until it becomes the sky.

ANNIVERSARY

You are dead.
The trees season in

and out of pleasure.
A blush of leaves

urge forward
from nothing.

The air opens,
brief as kindness

as the jacaranda
petal to the ground.

I am sick of being
out of touch with the living.

HOW TO DISAPPEAR

i
Water knows how to disappear,
how to empty itself into the sky.

It takes discipline, the emptying
isn't easy. She tries it
but her dumb ghost hands
keep moving.

ii
The ocean is always looking
for a way into her dreams.

She accepts whatever whispers by:
a flameback angel
a black box
revealing the details
of her disaster.

There are so many languages
in the ocean, so many
swallowed words.

iii
A wave breaks into the ocean,
becomes the ocean.

Each morning it rises,
newly formed, remembers
nothing.

THE SILENCE OF DOORWAYS

because the doorway is silent
and the window is thin as language
because the past just won't stop

because we rush away from silence
into speaking life, where mouths are mirrors
of one another and words flake off

I exhaled your name into a tree
let it settle

because the body heals in ways
the heart refuses, I whispered into that stone place
what did you think life would become?

ACKNOWLEDGMENTS

Grateful acknowledgment is given to the editors of the following publications in which these poems first appeared, sometimes in earlier versions:

Awosting Alchemy: "Numerosities" and "Now We Become Ghosts"

Bellevue Literary Review: "Poem of Denial," "Poem of Ego," "Poem of Eros and Thanatos" and "Poem of Undoing"

Chaparral: "Family Album," "Mother" and "Psychology 402: Brain and Behavior"

DecomP: "Ghost Brother"

Folly: "Poems of Submission," "The Flame" and "Three Exits"

Ghost Town: "Family Album" and "[untitled]"

Lily Literary Journal: "College Essay" and "Snapshots in Sepia"

Reed Magazine: "A May Elegy"

South Jersey Underground: "From a Bar in Elizabeth, New Jersey"

Spillway: "Disquietude"

Stirring: "A Brief Moment of Flight"

Transfer 88: "Meanwhile, an Obsession"

Two Hawks Quarterly: "Studying for the MCAT"

Wicked Alice: "Obsession"

I am tremendously grateful to the poetry community in Los Angeles which is a constant source of inspiration, most especially the members of Writers At Work who helped these poems through their many stages and whose encouragement, feedback, and friendship were instrumental in the completion of this book.

I am indebted to the following people for their support: Terry Wolverton, whose insight helped shape the book, Suzanne Lummis for her feedback and encouragement, Peggy Dobreer for her review and recommendation of the manuscript, and Eric Howard for his editorial assistance.

Many thanks to Dorothy Barresi, Chad Sweeney, and Roxane Beth Johnson for their support of this manuscript.

A very special thanks to Michael Miller and Moon Tide Press.

NOTES

“Meanwhile” is a collaging and twisting of words and lines pulled from various texts on feminist theory and literary theory, along with original lines.

“Submission to Your Touch” borrows a gesture from Deborah Landau.

“Abu Ghraib” and “Water Asks a Question” were inspired by Nick Flynn’s *The Captain Asks for a Show of Hands*. “Abu Ghraib” incorporates text from actual inmate testimonies.

“Mother” references Ted Kooser and Mary Oliver.

“Meanwhile, an Obsession” won the Mark Linenthal award at SFSU.

“Numerosities” was inspired by Lory Bedikian’s poem “Counting.”

In “Winter” the couplet in italics is from Robert Creeley’s “The Rain,” though slightly modified.

PATRONS

Moon Tide Press would like to thank the following people for their support in helping to publish the finest poetry from the Southern California region. To sign up as a patron, visit www.moontidepress.com or send an email to publisher@moontidepress.com.

GOLD PATRONS

Conner Brenner
Joely Khanh Linh Bui
Peggy Dobreer
S.A. Griffin
Michael Kramer
Lee Mallory
Robert and Michele Miller
Gabriella Miotto
Orange Lutheran High School
Rachanee Srisavasdi

PATRONS

Judith Remy Leder

ALSO AVAILABLE FROM MOON TIDE PRESS

Lost American Nights: Lyrics & Poems, Michael Ubaldini (2006)
Tide Pools: An Anthology of Orange County Poetry (2006)
Sleepyhead Assassins, Mindy Nettifee (2006)
A Thin Strand of Lights, Ricki Mandeville (2006)
Kindness from a Dark God, Ben Trigg (2007)
Carving in Bone: An Anthology of Orange County Poetry (2007)
A Wild Region, Kate Buckley (2008)
In the Heaven of Never Before, Carine Topal (2008)
Now and Then, Lee Mallory (2009)
Pop Art: An Anthology of Southern California Poetry (2010)
What We Ache For, Eric Morago (2010)
One World, Gail Newman (2011)
Hopeless Cases, Michael Kramer (2011)
I Was Building Up to Something, Susan Davis (2011)
In the Lake of Your Bones, Peggy Dobreer (2012)
Straws and Shadows, Irena Praitis (2012)
Cosmos: An Anthology of Southern California Poetry (2012)

CPSIA information can be obtained at www.ICGtesting.com
Printed in the USA
BVOW081122030313

314543BV00001B/8/P